Who's Your Candidate? Choosing Government Leaders

Becoming a STATE GOVERNOR

By Emily Mahoney

Gareth Stevens
PUBLISHING

Please visit our website, www.garethstevens.com. For a free color catalog of all our high-quality books, call toll free 1-800-542-2595 or fax 1-877-542-2596.

Library of Congress Cataloging-in-Publication Data

Mahoney, Emily Jankowski, author.
 Becoming a state governor / Emily Mahoney.
     pages cm. — (Who's your candidate? choosing government leaders)
 Includes index.
 ISBN 978-1-4824-4047-8 (pbk.)
 ISBN 978-1-4824-4048-5 (6 pack)
 ISBN 978-1-4824-4049-2 (library binding)
 1. Governors—United States—Juvenile literature. 2. State governments—United States—Juvenile literature. I. Title.
 JK2447.M24 2016
 352.23'21302373—dc23
                              2015021611

Published in 2016 by
Gareth Stevens Publishing
111 East 14th Street, Suite 349
New York, NY 10003

Designer: Andrea Davison-Bartolotta
Editor: Kristen Nelson

Photo credits: Cover, p. 1 (child) Leland Bobbe/Getty Images; cover, pp. 1 (office), 24–25 Nagel Photography/Shutterstock.com; p. 4 Francesco Dazzi/Shutterstock.com; p. 5 © iStockphoto.com/Steve Debenport; p. 6 John Leyba/The Denver Post/Getty Images; p. 8 Bloomberg/Getty Images; p. 9 Portland Press Herald/Getty Images; p. 11 Steve Pope/Getty Images; pp. 12–13 (main) Nabil K. Mark/Centre Daily Times/MCT/Getty Images; p. 13 (inset) IPGGutenbergUKLtd/iStock/Thinkstock; p. 14 Chris Clinton/Getty Images; p. 15 Chip Somodevilla/Getty Images; p. 16 Jupiterimages/Creatas/Thinkstock; p. 17 Nick White/Photodisc/Thinkstock; pp. 18–19 Dirk Anschutz/Getty Images; p. 20 hermosawave/iStock/Thinkstock; p. 21 Gerry Melendez/The State/MCT/Getty Images; p. 23 Jonathan Wiggs/The Boston Globe/Getty Images; p. 26 vadimguzhva/iStock/Thinkstock; p. 28 Goldnpuppy/Wikimedia Commons; p. 29 Diana Walker/Liasion Agency/Getty Images.

Printed in the United States of America

CPSIA compliance information: Batch #CW16GS: For further information contact Gareth Stevens, New York, New York at 1-800-542-2595.

CONTENTS

Words in the glossary appear in **bold** type the first time they are used in the text.

Making a Difference

Do you like being a leader? Perhaps you're the captain of your soccer team or have been in charge of planning a big event or project. What if you could make a career out of being a leader and making important decisions for your community? The state governor does just that!

You can be elected as a state governor and let your voice be heard to change the world you live in for the better. Being the leader of a club or captain of a sports team is much like doing that, so you may have a head start!

**State Capitol Building
Salt Lake City, Utah**

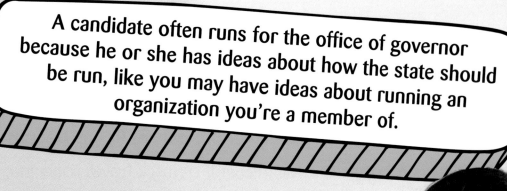

A candidate often runs for the office of governor because he or she has ideas about how the state should be run, like you may have ideas about running an organization you're a member of.

state Governor, Defined

A state governor is an elected official who's responsible for **implementing** state laws and making sure the state runs smoothly. The specific job of the governor varies from state to state, but all governors have command of the state's National Guard for **emergencies**.

Helping the Governor

A state governor is a powerful political figure because he or she is responsible for the well-being of everyone in a state. Each state has only one governor, and while their jobs have many things in common, some governors do things differently than others. The office of governor is unique, because governors can also choose how they want their staff to be organized.

Each governor has a chief of staff who is the go-to employee and who carries out a wide range of responsibilities, including managing office work and solving problems that come up. Without the chief of staff, the governor's office wouldn't run nearly as smoothly!

Organization Is Important!

There are three basic models for the organization of a governor's office:

- ⭐ strict **hierarchy** – all staff report to the governor through the chief of staff

- ☆ limited hierarchy – the chief of staff is in charge of most of the staff, but one or more other senior staff members answer directly to the governor in their areas of responsibility

- ✰ "spokes of the wheel" – some senior staff members report directly to the governor, and the governor gives direction as needed

Your Turn!

As a leader, you probably have a group or team member with whom you talk when making decisions. You trust this person because they know you very well and probably have similar ideas about how your organization should be run. Politicians need people like that on their staff, too!

In addition to the chief of staff, most states' governors have a lieutenant governor to look to for help. A person in this job deals with both the governor and the state **legislature** and is first in line to become governor should the governor be unable to fulfill his or her duties.

Becoming a Law

One of the governor's most important jobs is to take part in making state laws. The state legislature, the group of elected officials who write laws for a state, will submit a bill to the governor for his approval. If the governor doesn't like the bill or thinks it's unfair, the veto power can be used.

To "veto" means to "not allow." All 50 state governors have the power to veto a law for their state, but they must do so within a certain amount of time, or the bill automatically becomes a law. The length of this time period varies from state to state.

California governor Jerry Brown

All or Nothing?

A governor is able to veto an entire bill, but some governors also have the power to veto just parts of a bill. This means that if a governor likes most of a bill but dislikes a few points, he or she can call for the legislature to change or rework these items.

The legislature can often override a veto if a certain majority of its members vote to do so.

Who Can Run?

There are a few guidelines that determine who's **eligible** to run for state governor. Although each state has its own rules, here are a few examples. In New York, a person must be at least 30 years old and be a state **resident** for at least 5 years. The same is true in Mississippi. However, in California, there's no age requirement to become state governor!

All states require that candidates for governor live in the state and be legal citizens of the United States. This allows them to better represent the state they want to govern.

Take It to the Limit

Most terms for state governors are 4 years. In New Hampshire and Vermont, the governor only serves a 2-year term. In about three-quarters of US states, there is a limit on how many terms a governor can serve. In the other states, there is no limit on how many terms a governor can serve.

How Do They Get Elected?

The process of becoming a state governor can be long and confusing. Many people choose to run for governor after holding another type of smaller office, such as mayor or a member of the state legislature.

It's important for a **gubernatorial** candidate to travel to meet as many people as possible to get more votes and more money.

A gubernatorial candidate needs to campaign to get his or her name and ideas out to the public. Candidates make speeches to tell state residents what's important to them. They also convince people to contribute money to their campaign, because it can be very expensive. In fact, the combined cost of the top two candidates running for governor of Florida in 2014 was probably more than $150 million!

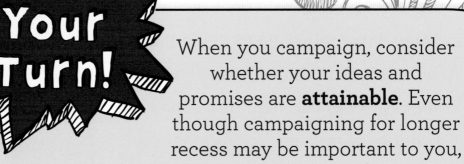

Your Turn!

When you campaign, consider whether your ideas and promises are **attainable**. Even though campaigning for longer recess may be important to you, if you cannot keep that promise, it may be wise to start with something more achievable, such as an extra field trip for your class.

The next step in an election for governor is to win the primary election. In the primary, members of the same political party run against each other. Since only one Democrat and one Republican can run for governor at a time, a candidate must first win their party's primary, and then he or she can run in the general election.

Once a candidate wins the primary, they get ready to run in the general election. That's when their campaign kicks into high gear. They'll be very busy over the coming months trying to beat the other candidates they're competing against since there can only be one governor in each state.

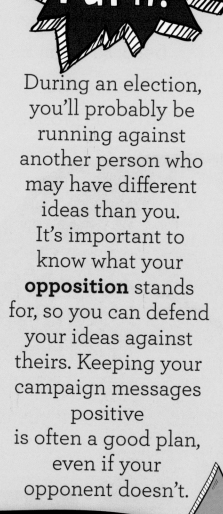

Your Turn!

During an election, you'll probably be running against another person who may have different ideas than you. It's important to know what your **opposition** stands for, so you can defend your ideas against theirs. Keeping your campaign messages positive is often a good plan, even if your opponent doesn't.

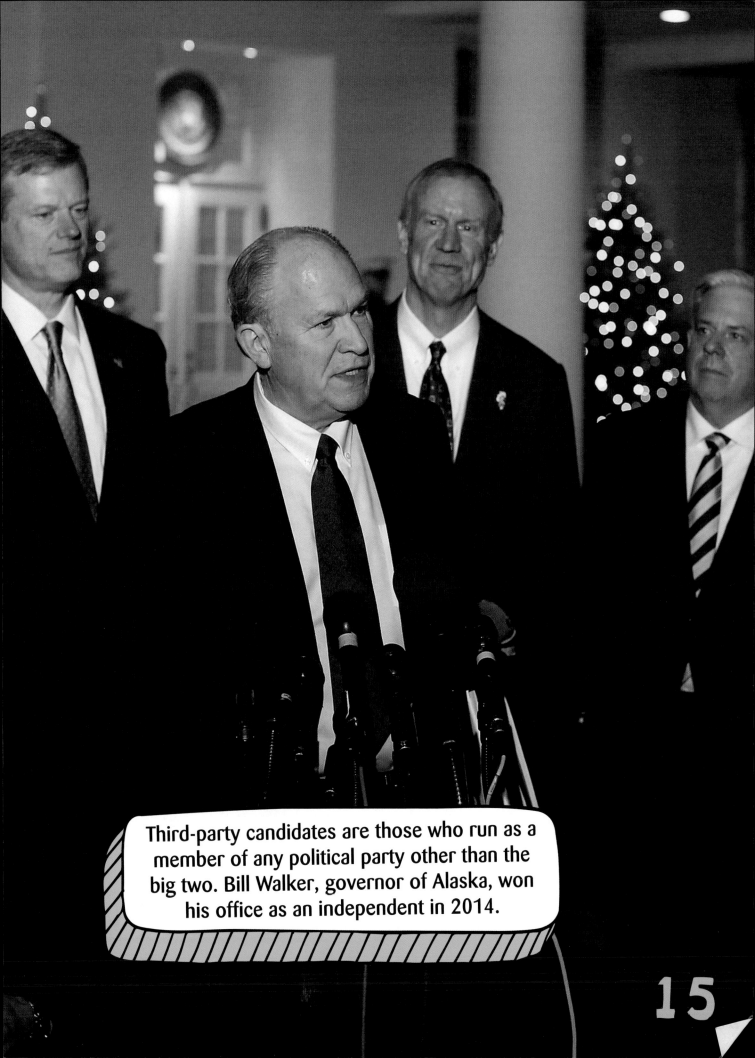

Third-party candidates are those who run as a member of any political party other than the big two. Bill Walker, governor of Alaska, won his office as an independent in 2014.

Your Campaign!

A lot can be learned from a state governor's campaign if you're planning to run for a student leadership position. First, just like the gubernatorial candidate must do, you should plan to attend many community or school events to meet many people. It's important to show that you support your voters so that they support you!

One way to reach new people is through social media. You may want to make a Facebook page or Twitter profile about your campaign to get your message to as many people as possible. This is also a nice reference page for people to go back to when they're deciding whom to vote for.

Your Turn!

A great place to start supporting your community is **volunteering** to help with community events. Check your local library or government office for a list of events looking for helpers. This way, you'll meet people who are interested in making a difference in your community!

Even politicians get nervous giving speeches! Practice any kind of speech you're giving, and think about how you would answer questions that people may ask about your campaign. This may help you be less nervous.

Just as most state governors have a lieutenant governor who helps make decisions, you may want to ask a friend to run for office with you. That way, your friend can help you make posters to advertise your campaign, help you reach more people, and support you when you have a question.

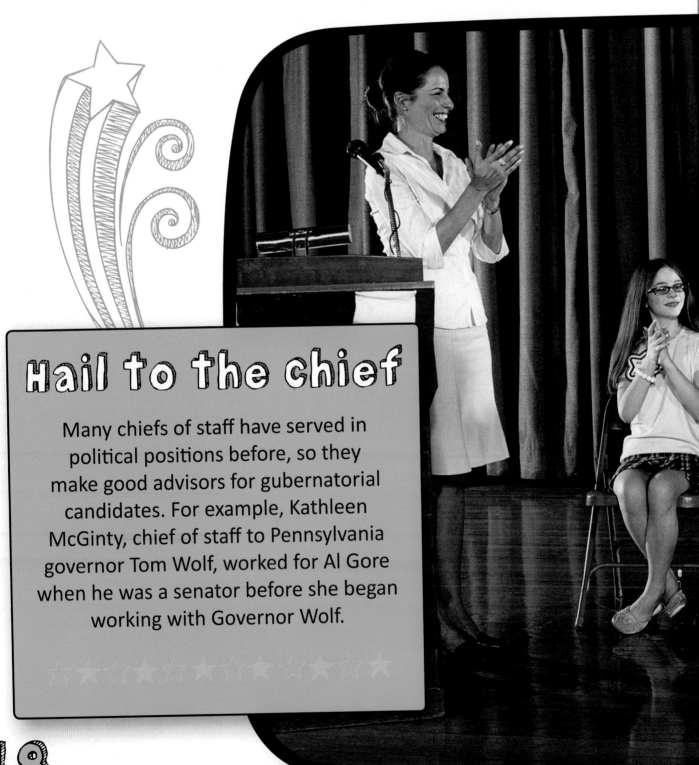

Hail to the chief

Many chiefs of staff have served in political positions before, so they make good advisors for gubernatorial candidates. For example, Kathleen McGinty, chief of staff to Pennsylvania governor Tom Wolf, worked for Al Gore when he was a senator before she began working with Governor Wolf.

It's always a good idea to involve a parent, teacher, or older community member in your campaign as well. They can help by making sure that your campaign promises are able to be completed, and they can also help with reaching a bigger (and more experienced) audience if you need to.

A good running mate would be organized, smart, and honest. It's important to have someone on your team who will always tell you the truth!

Time to Vote

The general election for governor takes place on Election Day, which is in November. Each voter can cast a vote for one person for governor. People often vote for the candidate who represents their political party, but they can choose to vote for whomever they want. They can even write someone's name on the ballot who isn't listed!

Some governors may be running for reelection. This means that they're currently the state governor and they want to continue holding office. It's up to the voters to decide if they'll stay in office, though!

A Big Year for Elections!

Every 4 years, there tend to be a lot of states that are electing a new governor. For example, in 2014, 36 states held gubernatorial elections, while only three states held gubernatorial elections in 2015. The year 2010 was another busy year when 37 gubernatorial elections were held.

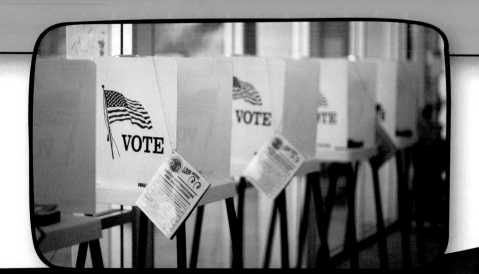

Someone who holds political office and is running to keep his or her position is called an incumbent. Governor of South Carolina Nikki Haley won as an incumbent in 2014.

Getting the Job Done

A state governor is a very busy person! Governors often travel throughout the state to meet with various government officials and see how things are running. They also visit areas where events that have caused suffering or loss have occurred to show their support for the victims.

Sometimes, a governor may even visit multiple cities in one day! A lot of time is spent on planes or driving, so a governor often uses travel time to get paperwork done. This **schedule** can be very demanding, but many governors say it's exciting to have something different to do every day.

Money Matters!

State governors are generally paid very well, but the amount they're paid varies from state to state. Maine is the lowest-paying state, with a yearly salary of $70,000, while the Pennsylvania state governor makes almost $190,000. Some governors refuse all or part of their salary to keep state costs low.

Often, the governor is asked to take part in an important event. Here, Massachusetts governor Deval Patrick (middle) participates in the ground breaking for the Edward M. Kennedy Institute for the United States Senate.

After the Election

In January, new governors take an **oath** of office. In it, they promise to support the Constitution, be faithful to the United States, and do their duties the best they can. Usually, the newly elected governor will give an **inaugural address** to the people of the state informing them what he or she plans to do during the term.

Your Turn!

Once you've been elected as a leader of an organization, it's important to look back at the promises you made while you were campaigning. It's your duty to do your best to make those promises come true. Taking small steps at the beginning of your term will help to ensure you build a strong organization. After all, you're the leader!

Some state governors have the added benefit of being able to live in the governor's mansion! These mansions are usually very beautiful and large, and the governor has a staff to take care of the house. Many mansions have public areas where people can come to see the beautiful architecture and fancy furniture.

GOVERNOR'S MANSION BUILT A.D. 1908

A TRIBUTE TO THE PEOPLE OF NEVADA
RESTORED
WHOSE GENEROSITY MADE POSSIBLE THIS RESTORATION IN 1963

The governor's family is invited to live with him or her in the mansion as well.

What Happens Next?

Many state governors go on to different political offices once their term is finished. The first governor to do this was the governor of Virginia, Thomas Jefferson, who went on to become the third president. More recently, George W. Bush, US president from 2001 to 2009, was the governor of Texas before he ran for president. Some governors also decide to run for **consecutive** terms, if this is allowed by their state.

However, many governors have a family. After their time in office, they may decide to retire from politics to spend more time with their children or to relax a bit after their busy schedule as governor.

Your Turn!

You may find that once you have successfully made changes in your organization, you want to have influence at a higher level. You can check your group's state or national organization to see if there are national meetings or events being held. You can simply attend them—or even help plan them!

Governors Who Became President

name	state governor of	gubernatorial term(s)	elected while governor
Thomas Jefferson	Virginia	1779–1781	No
James Monroe	Virginia	1799–1802	No
Martin Van Buren	New York	1829	No
John Tyler	Virginia	1825–1826	No
James K. Polk	Tennessee	1839–1841	No
Andrew Johnson	Tennessee	1853–1857	No
Rutherford B. Hayes	Ohio	1868–1872; 1876–1877	Yes
Grover Cleveland	New York	1883–1884	No
William McKinley	Ohio	1892–1896	Yes
Theodore Roosevelt	New York	1899–1900	Yes
Woodrow Wilson	New Jersey	1911–1913	Yes
Calvin Coolidge	Massachusetts	1919–1920	Yes
Franklin Roosevelt	New York	1929–1932	Yes
Jimmy Carter	Georgia	1971–1974	No
Ronald Reagan	California	1967–1974	No
Bill Clinton	Arkansas	1979–1980; 1983–1993	Yes
George W. Bush	Texas	1995–2000	Yes

Your Journey Starts Now!

There are many things that you can do now that will prepare you to run for state governor. First, paying attention in history and social studies classes is very important, so that you understand different parts of the government and how our nation is run. You can also take classes on public speaking or speech writing to prepare you to speak well in front of others.

Most importantly—keep working hard as the leader of your organization. The best way to practice leadership is to get real-life experience. The skills you learn while managing a group may one day help you make decisions for everyone in the state!

Start Young!

Michigan's first governor, Stevens Mason, was 23 years old when he was elected. He served from 1835 to 1840 and was responsible for having Michigan admitted as a state to the United States. His nickname was the "boy governor" because he was so young!

STEVENS T·MASON
· FIRST ·
GOVERNOR
OF MICHIGAN

Former president Bill Clinton was only 32 when he was elected governor of Arkansas!

GLOSSARY

attainable: able to be accomplished

consecutive: following one right after another

eligible: being qualified to do something

emergency: an unexpected situation that needs quick action

gubernatorial: having to do with the governor

hierarchy: the arrangement of people into levels based on their importance

implement: to put something into effect

inaugural address: the first speech someone makes when they take office

legislature: a lawmaking body in a state, county, or town

oath: a promise to uphold duties

opposition: competitor

resident: a person who lives somewhere on a long-term basis

schedule: a list of things that will be done and when they will be done

volunteer: to offer to do something willingly

FOR MORE INFORMATION

BOOKS

Machajewski, Sarah. *What Are State and Local Governments?* New York, NY: Britannica Educational Publishing, 2016.

Manning, Jack. *The State Governor.* North Mankato, MN: Capstone Press, 2015.

Thompson, Laurie Ann. *Be a Changemaker: How to Start Something That Matters.* New York, NY: Simon Pulse, 2014.

WEBSITES

Contact Your State Governor
www.usa.gov/Contact/Governors.shtml
Use this website to contact your governor about ideas you have for your state!

How State Governors Work
people.howstuffworks.com/government/local-politics/state-Governor1.htm
Find out important information about becoming a state governor.